KITTENS
Need Someone to Love

By P. Mignon Hinds
Illustrated by Alan Phillips

A GOLDEN BOOK, New York
Western Publishing Company, Inc.
Racine, Wisconsin 53404

Text copyright © 1981 by Western Publishing Company, Inc. Illustrations copyright © 1981 by Alan Phillips.
All rights reserved. Printed in the U.S.A. No part of this book may be reproduced or copied in any form without
written permission from the publisher GOLDEN®, GOLDEN® & DESIGN, A GOLDEN LOOK-LOOK® BOOK, and A GOLDEN BOOK®
are trademarks of Western Publishing Company, Inc.
Library of Congress Catalog Card Number: 80-84785
ISBN 0-307-11865-7/ISBN 0-307-61865-X (lib. bdg.)   H I J

Kittens are clever, curious, lovable baby animals.

To grow up strong and happy, kittens need many things.

Newborn kittens need their mother
to love them and take care of them.

Kittens should stay with their mother
until they are at least six weeks old.

When kittens get older, they need
a comfortable place of their own.

Kittens take many naps. They need plenty of rest.
A sleepy kitten should have a warm, soft bed.

Kittens have little stomachs. Hungry kittens
need small meals several times each day.

Kittens can get very
thirsty. They should have
a bowl that is always filled
with fresh, clean water.

Kittens who stay indoors must learn to use a litter pan.
It should always be kept clean and dry.

Kittens do not need to be bathed.
They lick themselves clean.

But kittens should be brushed often so they won't swallow loose hairs. Hairs in their stomach can make them sick.

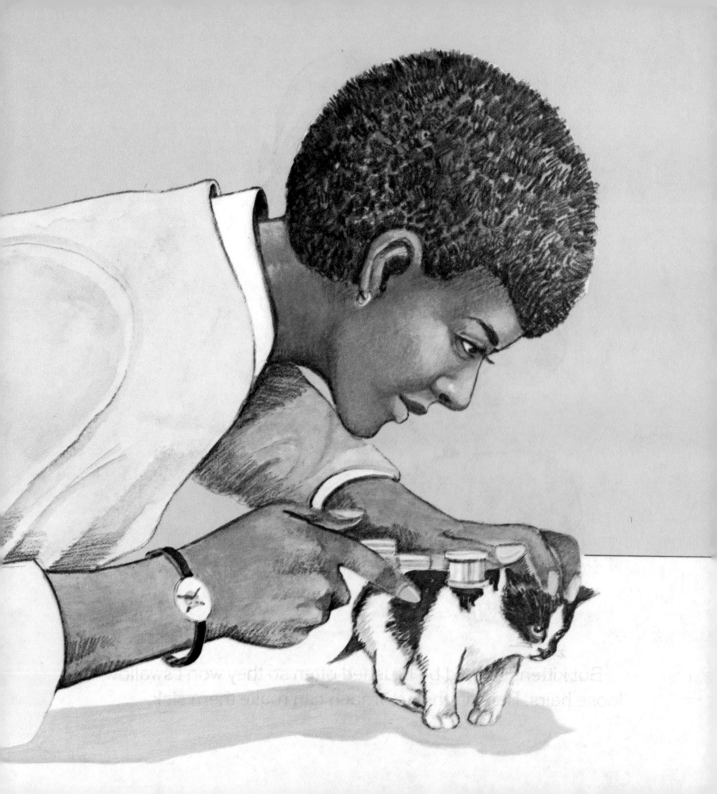

Kittens need an animal
doctor to give them checkups
and take care of them when
they are not well.

Country kittens need a safe place to run and play.

In cities and towns, kittens are happier indoors.
When traveling outdoors, a kitten should be kept
in a cat carrier.

Kittens love to pounce and play and scratch.
They dig their sharp little claws into everything.

Kittens need kitty toys to play with,
and a scratching post or an old scrap of rug
so they won't scratch the furniture.

Naughty kittens
need to be told when
they have done
something wrong.

Sweet little kittens should be told
when they do the right thing.
     A gentle cuddle is a good way to say,
"You are the best kitten in the world."

Kittens need cuddling and scolding and protecting.

Kittens need to eat and sleep and play.

But most of all, kittens
need someone to love.